This book belongs to

SYLVIA PLATH

The It-Doesn't-Matter Suit

illustrations by Rotraut Susanne Berner

faber and faber
LONDON · BOSTON

First published in Great Britain in 1996
by Faber and Faber Limited
3 Queen Square London WC1N 3AU

Printed in England by BPC Hazell Books Ltd, Aylesbury,
Buckinghamshire

A CIP record for this book
is available from the British Library

ISBN 0–571–16613–X

2 4 6 8 10 9 7 5 3 1

The It-Doesn't-Matter Suit

Max Nix was seven years old, and the youngest of seven brothers. First came Paul, the eldest and tallest of all seven. Then came Emil. Then Otto and Walter, and Hugo and Johann.

Paul   Emil   Otto   Walter

Last came Max. Max's whole name was Maximilian, but because he was only seven he did not need such a big name. So everybody called him just Max.

Hugo   Johann   Max   Cat

Max lived with Mama and Papa Nix and his six brothers in a little village called Winkelburg, halfway up a steep mountain. The mountain had three peaks, and on all three peaks, winter and summer, sat caps of snow like three big scoops of vanilla ice-cream. On nights when the moon rose round and bright as an orange balloon you could hear the foxes barking in the dark pine forest high above Max's house. On clear, sunlit days you could see the river winking and blinking far, far below in the valley, small and thin as a silver ribbon.

Max liked where he lived.

Max was happy, except for one thing.

More than anything else in the world Max Nix wanted a suit of his own.

He had a green sweater and green wool socks and a green felt hunting hat with a turkey feather in it. He even had a fine pair of leather knickers with carved bone buttons. But everybody knows a sweater and a pair of knickers are not the same thing as a suit – a made-to-order suit with long trousers and a jacket to match.

Wherever Max Nix looked in Winkelburg – east and west, north and south, high and low and round about – he saw people wearing suits. Some people had suits for work, and these were very sturdy suits of brown or grey cloth. Some people had suits for weddings, and these were very handsome suits with striped silk waistcoats. Some people had suits for

skiing, and these were gay blue or red suits with rows of snowflakes or edelweiss embroidered on the cuffs and collars.

Some people had summer suits of linen, white and crisp as letter paper. Papa Nix and Paul and Emil and Otto and Walter and Hugo and Johann all had suits. *Everybody* on the mountain had some sort of suit except Max.

Now Max did not want a suit *just* for work
   (that would be too plain)
or *just* for weddings
   (that would be too fancy)
or *just* for skiing
   (that would be too hot)
or *just* for summer
   (that would be too cool).
He wanted a suit for All-Year-Round.
He wanted a suit for doing Everything.
Not too plain a suit for birthdays and holidays,
and not too fancy a suit for school and calling the
cows home. Not too hot a suit for hiking in July, and
not too cool a suit for coasting in the snow.

If Max had a suit for All-Year-Round, the butcher
and the baker, and the blacksmith and the gold-
smith, and the tinker and the tailor, and the inn-
keeper and the schoolteacher, and the grocer and the
goodwives, and the minister and the mayor, and
everybody else in Winkelburg would flock to their
doors and windows when he went by. 'Look!' they
would murmur to one another. 'There goes
Maximilian in his marvellous suit!'

If Max had a suit for doing Everything, the cats in the alleys and the dogs on the cobbles of Winkelburg would follow him uptown and downtown, purring and grrring with admiration.

That was the sort of suit Max was dreaming about the day the postman of Winkelburg knocked on the Nixes' door and delivered the big package.

The package was shaped like a long, flattish box.

It was wrapped round with heavy brown wrapping paper.

It was tied with red string.

Across the top of the package Max spelled out N-I-X in large black letters. The first name had been rained on and not even the Postmaster of Winkelburg could read it. So nobody knew *which* Nix the package was for.

The package might be for Papa Nix, or Paul or Emil, or Otto or Walter, or Hugo or Johann. It might even be for Max. Nobody could tell for sure.

Mama Nix had just baked a batch of apricot tarts. Everybody sat around the kitchen table, wondering who the package was for, and who it was from, and what was in it, and eating up the apricot tarts one by one.

It was not Christmastime, so it was not a Christmas present.

It was not near anybody's birthday, so it was not a birthday present.

'It is too short,' said Paul, 'to be a pair of skis.'

'It is too small,' said Emil, 'to be a toboggan.'

'It is too light,' said Otto, lifting the package easily, 'to be a bicycle.'

'It is too wide,' said Walter, 'to be a fishing rod.'

'It is too large,' said Hugo, 'to be a hunting knife.'

Johann put his ear to the package and gave it a little shake. 'It is too quiet,' he said, 'to be a cow bell.'

Max did not say anything. It is too fine, he thought to himself, to be for me.

At last the apricot tarts were all gone, and still nobody could guess what was in the package.

'Let us open it,' everybody said.

Papa Nix untied the knot in the red string. Mama Nix unwrapped the brown paper. Inside the brown paper was a grey cardboard box. Paul lifted the lid off the box. Inside the grey box was a lot of white tissue paper. Emil and Otto and Walter and Hugo and Johann and Max all helped to pull away some of the tissue paper.

And there in the grey box with a wreath of white
tissue paper around it lay a
>woolly
>whiskery
>brand-new
>mustard-yellow
>suit
>>with three brass
buttons shining like mirrors on the front of it, and
two brass buttons at the back, and a brass button on
each cuff.

'What a strange suit,' said Papa Nix. 'I have never
seen anything quite like it.'

'It is made of good strong cloth,' said Mama Nix,
feeling the yellow wool between thumb and fore-
finger. '*This* suit will not wear out in a hurry.'

'It is a handsome suit!' said Paul.

'Light as a feather!' said Emil.

'Bright as butter!' said Otto.

'Warm as toast!' said Walter.

'Simply fine!' said Hugo.

'Dandy!' said Johann.

'O my!' said Max.

Every one of the seven brothers wished he owned
just such a suit.

But the suit looked as if it might be Papa Nix's size. So Papa Nix tried it on. The jacket was wide enough, and the trousers were long enough. The suit fitted Papa Nix to a T.

'I shall wear the suit to work tomorrow,' he said.

Papa Nix worked in a bank. He thought how it would be to wear the woolly, whiskery, brand-new, mustard-yellow suit to work. Such a suit had never been seen before in all Winkelburg. What would the people say? Perhaps they would think the suit was too gay for a sensible banker. Those brass buttons would flash out like big coins. All the other bankers wore dark blue or dark grey suits. None of them ever wore a mustard-yellow suit.

At last Papa Nix sighed and said, 'I am too big to wear a mustard-yellow suit.'

Paul held his breath.

'I will give the suit to Paul,' said Papa Nix.

So Paul tried on the mustard-yellow suit. Paul was as tall as Papa Nix, so the trousers were the right length. He was not as broad as Papa Nix around the middle though, so the jacket hung about him in loose, flapping folds. But Mama Nix was clever with needle and thread. She took a tuck here and a stitch there. When she was through, the suit fitted Paul to a T.

'I shall wear the suit skiing tomorrow,' he said.

Paul often went skiing with his friends. He thought how it would be to wear the woolly, whiskery, brand-new, mustard-yellow suit skiing. Such a suit had never been seen before in all Winkelburg. What would his friends say? Perhaps they would think yellow was a silly colour for a ski-suit. He would look like a meadow of sunflowers against the snow. All his friends wore red ski-suits or blue ski-suits. None of them ever wore a mustard-yellow suit.

At last Paul sighed and said, 'I, also, am too big to wear a mustard-yellow suit.'

Emil held his breath.

'Let Emil try on the suit,' said Paul.

So Emil tried on the mustard-yellow suit. Emil was as broad as Paul, but shorter. The cuffs of the jacket covered his hands, and the cuffs of the trousers folded down over his shoes. But Mama Nix took a tuck here and a stitch there. When she was through the suit fitted Emil to a T.

'I shall wear the suit in the toboggan race tomorrow,' he said.

Emil was a member of the Winkelburg toboggan team. Once a month the Winkelburg team raced the team of the town on the other side of the mountain. He thought how it would be to wear the woolly, whiskery, brand-new, mustard-yellow suit in the toboggan races. Such a suit had never been seen before in all Winkelburg. What would his team-mates say? Perhaps they would think he was trying to show off in the mustard-yellow suit. He would look like a streak of lightning going down the toboggan track. All his team-mates wore brown zipper-jackets and brown pants. None of them ever wore a mustard-yellow suit.

At last Emil sighed and said, 'I, also, am too big to wear a mustard-yellow suit.'

Otto held his breath.

'Maybe the suit will be right for Otto,' said Emil.

So Otto tried on the mustard-yellow suit. Otto was almost as tall as Emil, only his shoulders were not quite so broad. The jacket drooped a little. But Mama Nix took a tuck here and a stitch there. When she was through the suit fitted Otto to a T.

'I shall wear the suit on my paper round tomorrow,' he said.

Otto delivered newspapers on his bicycle. He thought how it would be to wear the woolly, whiskery, brand-new, mustard-yellow suit on his paper round. Such a suit had never been seen before in all Winkelburg. What would his customers say? Perhaps they would think the suit was too fancy for a paperboy. He might splash mud on it or be caught in the rain, and then what a sorry sight he would be. All the other paperboys wore their old clothes when they delivered papers. None of them ever wore a brand-new, mustard-yellow suit.

At last Otto sighed and said, 'I, also, am too big to wear a mustard-yellow suit.'

Walter held his breath.

'If the suit fits me, it should fit Walter,' said Otto.

So Walter tried on the mustard-yellow suit. Walter was a little shorter than Otto, and a little thinner. But Mama Nix took a tuck here and a stitch there and moved the brass buttons over an inch. When she was through the suit fitted Walter to a T.

'I shall wear the suit ice-fishing tomorrow,' he said.

Walter often went ice-fishing in Winkelburg Lake in the winter. He thought how it would be to wear the woolly, whiskery, brand-new, mustard-yellow suit ice-fishing. Such a suit had never been seen before in all Winkelburg. What would the fish think? Perhaps the suit would frighten them away. It would glow through the ice like a bright sun. The other fishermen all wore green suits in the summer so the fish could not tell them from leaves, and brown suits in the winter so the fish could not tell them from tree trunks. None of them ever wore a mustard-yellow suit.

At last Walter sighed and said, 'I, also, am too big to wear a mustard-yellow suit.'

Hugo held his breath.

'Perhaps Hugo might like to wear it,' said Walter.

So Hugo tried on the mustard-yellow suit. Hugo was a good deal shorter than Walter, but Mama Nix snipped a bit here and trimmed a bit there with her scissors and turned the thread-ends under. When she was through the suit fitted Hugo to a T.

'I shall wear the suit hunting tomorrow,' he said.

Hugo often went fox-hunting in the forest above Winkelburg, for the foxes stole the plump Winkelburg chickens. He thought how it would be to wear the woolly, whiskery, brand-new, mustard-yellow suit fox-hunting. Such a suit had never been seen before in all Winkelburg. What would the fox think? Perhaps the fox would just hide in a hole and laugh at him. The brass buttons would beam like lanterns from far off and warn the fox he was coming. All the other hunters wore checked and speckled suits so the fox could not see them easily in the checked and speckled shade of the forest. None of them ever wore a mustard-yellow suit.

At last Hugo sighed and said, 'I, also, am too big to wear a mustard-yellow suit.'

Johann held his breath.

'Let's see how the suit looks on Johann,' said Hugo.

So Johann tried on the mustard-yellow suit. Johann was shorter and rounder than Hugo, but Mama Nix snipped here and clipped there and moved the buttons back to the edge of the jacket. When she was through the suit fitted Johann to a T.

'I shall wear the suit for milking the cows tomor-row,' he said.

Johann took turns with his six brothers milking Papa Nix's cows. He thought how it would be to wear the woolly, whiskery, brand-new, mustard-yellow suit for milking the cows. Such a suit had never been seen before in all Winkelburg. What would the cows think? Perhaps they would take him for a bundle of whiskery yellow hay and nibble at his collar. Everybody else wore blue overalls for milking cows. Nobody ever wore a mustard-yellow suit.

At last Johann sighed and said, 'Even I am too big to wear a mustard-yellow suit.'

Max could hardly keep from jumping up and down, but he held still as a mouse and waited to see what would happen.

'Max has no suit,' said Johann.

'Goodness!' said Papa Nix.

'Gracious!' said Mama Nix.

'Let it be Max's suit,' everybody said, nodding and smiling.

So Max tried on the mustard-yellow suit. Max was the shortest and thinnest of all the Nix brothers, but Mama Nix snipped and stitched and took tucks and moved buttons. When she was through the suit fitted Max as if it were made-to-order.

'I shall wear the suit,' Max said, 'today and tomorrow and the day after that.'

Max went to school in his mustard-yellow suit. He walked straight and he sat tall, and pretty soon the schoolchildren began to wish they had suits like the suit Max wore. So even though nobody in Winkelburg had ever seen such a suit before
IT DIDN'T MATTER.

Max went skiing in his mustard-yellow suit. He slipped and slid for a way on the seat of his pants, but the cloth of the suit was very strong and didn't rip, so
IT DIDN'T MATTER.

Max rode his bicycle in his mustard-yellow suit.
He got caught in the rain, but the drops ran right off
the whiskery suit like drops off a duck's back, so
IT DIDN'T MATTER.

Max went ice-fishing in his mustard-yellow suit. The fish came swimming up to see what gleamed so bright on the other side of the ice, and Max caught enough for supper. He got some fish scales on his suit, but everybody was so busy admiring Max's fish that they never noticed, so
IT DIDN'T MATTER.

Max went coasting in his mustard-yellow suit. He tipped over once or twice and landed in a cold snowbank, but the woolly suit was very warm, so
IT DIDN'T MATTER.

Max went fox-hunting in his mustard-yellow suit. The fox saw something yellow through the trees and thought it was a fat, yellow Winkelburg chicken. His mouth started to water and he came running. Max caught the fox. He lost a brass button in the bushes, but the button shone out like a star in the dark forest and he found it again, so

IT DIDN'T MATTER.

Max milked the cows in his mustard-yellow suit. The suit's sunny colour made the cows dream of buttercups and daisies in the spring meadows, and they mooed for happiness. When Max finished milking he had three pails full of the creamiest milk ever

seen in Winkelburg. Some pieces of hay stuck to the suit, but the hay was yellow and the suit was yellow and the hay didn't show, so

IT DIDN'T MATTER.

Max walked uptown and downtown and round about Winkelburg in his mustard-yellow suit. When he went by, the butcher and the baker, the blacksmith and the goldsmith, the tinker and the tailor, the innkeeper and the schoolteacher, the grocer and the goodwives, the minister and the mayor all leaned out of their doors and windows.

'Look!' they murmured to one another. 'There goes Maximilian in his marvellous suit.'

And the cats in the alleys and the dogs on the cobbles of Winkelburg followed at his heels, purring and grrring with admiration for Max Nix and his
    wonderful
    woolly
    whiskery
    brand-new
    mustard-yellow
    IT-DOESN'T-MATTER SUIT.